Mixed Emotions

Beryl Victoria Francis

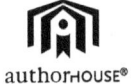

authorHOUSE®

AuthorHouse™ LLC
1663 Liberty Drive
Bloomington, IN 47403
www.authorhouse.com
Phone: 1-800-839-8640

Published by AuthorHouse 03/26/2014

ISBN: 978-1-4918-4992-7 (sc)
ISBN: 978-1-4918-4991-0 (e)

Library of Congress Control Number: 2014900736

Any people depicted in stock imagery provided by Thinkstock are models,
and such images are being used for illustrative purposes only.
Certain stock imagery © Thinkstock.

This book is printed on acid-free paper.

"I can do all things through Christ which strengthen me."
(Phillippians 4:13)

Introduction

On May 17, 2013, I decided to turn the lyrics the Lord gave me for songs into a book of poems. Reason is I have a CD with twelve songs, (one I made from psalms 50) my own lyrics and my own tunes. I tried very hard even to get the CD air played, but with no luck. I cannot sit on these words that the Lord helped me to put on paper. I want them to go out into the world that souls can be drawn closer to God.

So, here is my book of poems written from 2005-2013. Read everyone and be blessed.

Contents

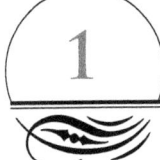

The Agony and the Pain

Lord Jesus you left your glory above
you walked on this sinful earth among men
you do all the good you can. You feed, you heal,
you teach and you save, and then you died on Calvary's Cross!
Oh the agony and the pain you bear. Thank you Lord for
dying for me

Jesus you came to sinful earth
you know your destiny but you came anyhow.
The agony and the pain you bear
You became sin for us, it's just because you love us so
Father thank you for sending your son to die. Thank you
Jesus for dying for me

Lord Jesus Gethesename was where you prayed
Your sweat became drops of blood on the ground
They beat you all the way to Calvary, the cruel
Shameful death you die. Our sins nailed you to the cross!
Oh, the agony and the pain you bear. Thank you Lord
Jesus for dying for me.

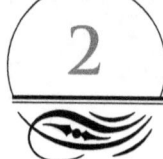

He'll be enough for me

When problems come my way
loved ones and friends forsake me
my God is enough for me. Though the
way seem dark and dreary, I just know
he is my stay. My God is enough for me

He'll be enough for me no matter
what's the problem by his grace I will
conquer them. In my needs I can call on him
and he will supply them in his own time. I know
my God is enough for me

Enough, enough, I know my God is enough for me
sometimes I feel so discourage, but on my knees I go
and there I found the answer, he is always near. My God
is enough for me.

It's just because of you

Oh my God I thank you for sending your only son
to die for sinful man. Thank you for saving grace. Our
sins are the reason why you were nailed to Calvary's
cross. You bear the shame for us all. Thank you Jesus
for your love

Oh father thank you for letting your son go
Thank you Jesus for your willingness to come
to earth to die, to save a sinner like me.
The entire human race would be lost
What would we do Lord without you
Jesus, its just because of you

Sometimes Lord I just want to praise and
glorify you, just to lift up my hands to heaven
without asking you for a thing. Please help me to
praise your name. You have done so much
for the souls of man. Thank you Lord for coming
to earth. It's just because of you.

God is Watching You

God is watching you. God is watching you.
He is always near, no matter what you say,
no matter what you do, my God is watching you
You cannot hide from him. He is watching you
Dark and light is the same to him

He is the God of the light. He is watching you.
He can see through the dark. He is watching you.
Be conscious of his presence. He is watching you.
He hears all you say. He sees all you do. He is
watching you.

Keep your mind on the Lord. He is watching you.
Your mind can be your greatest friend and it can be
your greatest foe. Trust God and relax, he is watching
you, he is watching you.

All is Thine

O father you created this world and all that is there in.
A thousand cattle on the hills are thine, silver and gold
is thine. When we give to thy cause, we give thee but
thine own, all is thine.

Lord, Satan want to have us bound, but you send your
son to die to loose us from the bond of sin. We are thine
and all that we have is yours. Help us to freely give.

Lord, you created man to worship you, but man has
turned away from you and broken your holy laws.
We are on borrowed times and all that we have
O Lord is thine.

The Blood of Jesus

The Father sent his only son to die on Calvary,
Jesus is his name. His precious blood was shed
for you and me, he died on Calvary. Jesus is just
a breadth away, call on him, he will save you
that's why he came.

The precious blood of Jesus, the blood,
the blood of Jesus. There is healing in his
blood, there is power in his blood. There is
salvation through his blood. The blood will
never loose its power. Call on him he will
answer you.

Plea the blood of Jesus in faith for healing,
healing you will receive. Plea the blood for the protection,
protection you will receive. Plea the blood against
the hand of the enemy, trust in Jesus, believe on him,
your needs he will supply.

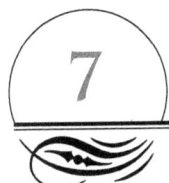

The sweet Name of Jesus

Jesus is the sweetest name I know
I love to sing his praise. He is always
the same if you just learn to know him.
He will be your friend in time of despair,
loneliness and fear! Jesus is the sweetness
name I know.

Jesus, I love his name. I love I love his name.
Precious Jesus there is no other name I know.
I lift up my voice above to sing your praise!
O the sweet name of Jesus, the sweetest name
I know.

O my friends come to Jesus today, you will find
the comfort of his love. O the fragrance of his
presence, learn to call on him, his mercy will save
you, trust in him today. Jesus the sweetest name
I know.

The Coming Christ

Jesus is coming again, it seems as if he tarry long,
but you are saved my friends. You should be glad
he is not here yet, for if you are not ready when he
comes it would have been better if you were not born.

It will be a weeping and a wailing when Christ comes
O sinner man. Don't be getting ready my friends, get
ready, get ready, get ready. This is no joke; he is coming
soon! Make your choice to come to Jesus today.

Please do not delay this invitation
Christ wounded hands are stretched
out still. The call is urgent, now is the
day, the day salvation. Don't put it off
 for another day. Jesus is waiting for you
to make the move.

My Song of Praise

Your saving grace o Lord will always be my
song of praise. Lord, you gave us grace that we
don't even deserve! While we were your enemies
you die for us on Calvary. That's why I have to
praise you Lord.

Worthy, worthy is the lamb, you are worthy of our
praise. I just praise your holy name for saving grace.
What would we do without you Lord. Thank you for
your love. You are worthy, you are worthy of your praise

I lift up my song, my song of praise with all my heart
to glorify your holy name. Worthy are you Lord to
receive praise. Thank you oh Lord for saving grace. Thank
you for your love. I love to sing your praise.

Do You Know Him

The father sent his only son to die for the sins of this whole world. His name is Jesus, do you know him. We should have died on the cross, but he pay the price for us all, he died in our place. Do you know him

When we should have been destroyed, Jesus said to the father, my blood, my blood I died for them. He is the same today. Jesus is calling you now, give up your sins and surrender to him, and try to know him.

Jesus hands are stretched out still calling sinners to come home. Do you know him? His love for you will never end. His eyes are watching you both in the light and in the dark. Come to Jesus now, then you will know him.

The Holy Spirit of God

The holy spirit of God hear us now while we
sing, pouring out your holy spirit all over us
we pray. Holy spirit the comforter send from
God above stay right here with us and bless us
now we pray

Jesus, you said if you don't go away the
Holy Spirit will not come. Holy Spirit, you
are here, we adore you now. Thank you Lord
for the gift, the gift of the holy spirit, do thy
work O Lord in us now we pray

The Holy Spirit of God, here we are today
We humble beseech thee anoint us now
we pray, pouring it out all over us, we
welcome thee now. Sweet spirit of God
cleanse us now we pray.

Lord I can count on you

Lord I can count on you I can count on you
You know all about me. You wake me up this
morning and set me on my way. That's why I
know I can count on you, you never fail me yet

Every breadth I take, every step I make
I can count on you. So Lord, please hold
my hand lest I'll fall. Lord, please remind
me that you are just a breadth away, and
I can pray.

My wonderful Lord, my precious saviour
you are my provider. Sometimes things
don't go the way I want them, but I know
you give to your children what suite
them best

Dear Lord I am nothing without you
Please give me the faith to wait on you
If I only wait on you Lord I know all
my needs will be met. I put all my faith
in you for I know I can count on you.

Give me that will

There is a secret that the Lord has given man
that is hidden from old Satan, and that is our
will. Satan can only have it if we give it to him.
Our will is to either serve the Lord or Satan, and
that is the choice we all have to make.

Jesus is saying give me that will,
don't allow Satan to control it. I will
take possession of it to do my good
pleasure in you. Our five senses are the
devil's play ground, run him away and
let Jesus take control of your will

Don't make it easy for Satan to have your will.
Plea the blood of Jesus on him and run him away.
Satan wants to have your will, don't give it to him.
As long as Christ have control of your life, Satan is
powerless. Jesus is saying give me that will today.

The Holy Name of Jesus

Holy Holy is your name O Lord,
everything about you is holy. Lord
you said you are holy and we must be
holy. Please help us to strive towards
holiness because without holiness we
cannot see you. Holy Holy O Lord
is thy name.

I love to sing about you Lord, for there
is none like you, holy is thy name. When
we are in your presence we are standing on
holy ground. Please help us to love and fear
thee and be conscious of thy presence.

O the holy name of Jesus no sin cannot
enter the courts of heaven for heaven is
a holy place. O Jesus holy is your name
help us to fear and trust thee for thou art
holy. O Lord holy is thy name.

The Lovely Name of Jesus

O the name, the name of Jesus, what a lovely name.
Great is thy name, thy name O Lord thrills my very
Soul and makes me want to sing, to sing of thee always
Jesus! Jesus! Oh what a lovely name

Help me dear Jesus to take time out daily to talk about
you to sing about you. There is strength in your name
power in your name, love, joy, and peace in your name
O what a lovely name, hallelujah what a lovely name

O the precious name of Jesus, what a lovely name
If you are sick, you can call on him. There is healing
in his name. If you are lonely, call on him, there is
comfort in his name. Jesus Jesus what a lovely name

Don't Let me go

O Lord I am weak but thou art strong
hold my hand don't let me go
Hold my hand lest I'll fall and I'll
go by the side of the road. Please Jesus
don't let me go, don't let me go

Lord when we do the right the devil
is mad and even strike at us and knock
us down. I am glad you are always there
to pick us up when we fall. Precious Jesus
don't let me go.

Though the road seems dark and dreary,
Lord Jesus I know I can depend on thee,
don't let me go. You are my comforter and
my friend, there is no one like you
don't let me go.

When Probation is closed

Listen my friends listen closely, now is the time for us to be saved. Jesus is patiently calling you now. Probation soon will be closed. Be saved today, for no sin cannot enter the courts of heaven. Come to Jesus today, he will receive you.

When probation is closed there is no time for repentance. Don't you know the Lord rather not the death of the sinner, but that he may turn from his wickedness and live. accept the Lord today he will not turn you away.

This is the day of salvation, be saved today. There is a message in every song and this is my message to you. Run, run for your life, Jesus is coming soon, he is tenderly calling you now don't delay for another day.

Don't walk away

You may say this world is in a bad state, so many people are dying every day. People killing themselves, people dying for hunger, people killing each other. Nations fighting against nations. If there is a God, why are these things happening.

Believe it or not my friends, there is a God Don't walk away. When Jesus died on the Cross, God was right there, don't walk away Jesus loves you, don't you walk away just lean on him and trust him, he is always near.

So you see sin is the cause of these things don't blame God. If you have problems in your life, don't give up, just whisper a prayer to God he will take care of you just learn to trust him my friend don't walk away.

Flying without wings

As I put my trust in you Lord,
as I read your holy words
as I learn more of you, your
holy words are so true to me
I feel am flying without wings
Your love is so strong. Thank you
for your love for man. I feel am
flying without wings.

Right now I feel am flying without wings
Am so grateful am so happy in thee Lord
I feel am souring through the skies. Thank
you father for sending your son to sinful earth
to save us from our sins. Am flying without wings

My Lord is so good, so good to me
He is so sweet. I love him because he
first loves me. Jesus, if I was the only sinner
on earth, you would come and die for me. Lord
when I think of your greatness and your love, I
feel am flying without wings.

If I have wings like a dove

When burdens are heavy, I said Lord,
if I have wings like a dove, I would fly
away and be at rest, but I know I have a
savior who I can trust. Since I have no wings
I will just stay here and sing, sing, sing.

If I have wings like a dove, I would soar through
the skies far away and be at rest. I know I have a
savior that I can lean on. He never fails me yet, so
since I have no wings, I'll stay down here and
sing, sing, sing.

My friends, our God never makes a mistake
He made every thing good in his own time.
He never made us with wings. He knows the
trouble we would give in the sky. All prospect
please God only man is vile, so I'll stay here
and sing, sing, sing.

A second chance

Thank you Lord that you give us a second chance.
When we sin and fall so bad, you never throw us away
We are the ones that stray from you. You never leave us
alone. Thank you Lord! Thank you for a second chance

Thank you Lord! Thank you for a second chance.
You are so merciful, so kind, so loving and so true
You watch over us night and day. Please help us
not to take anything for granted. Thank you for a
second chance

O Lord Jesus we wondered away from thee so
many times. Your wounded hands are stretched
out still, calling us to come back to you. You are
always there to pick us up when we fall. Thank
you Lord for a second chance.

How beautiful heaven must be

How beautiful heaven must be, the
father, son, the holy ghost and all the
heavenly host. Just imagine the clean
atmosphere, the praises and the adoration!
To our maker and our king
God's beautiful heaven of rest

O how beautiful heaven must be, in the
home of the bless, in the mansion of rest.
Sweet home of God's eternal rest no sin
cannot enter that beautiful place. The streets
are of pure gold. God's beautiful heaven of rest.

I heard of that mansion Christ gone to prepare
There is no night there. Jesus is the light and he
is coming soon. He is coming for his own and by
his grace I'll be where he is. God's beautiful heaven
of rest.

Am Waiting

Lord am waiting, am waiting, am waiting
for my blessings. You promise me if I wait
you will bless me. The word said, wait on the
Lord and he will strengthen thine heart. Am
waiting Lord your words are so true. Please
help me to wait for I am waiting on you.

O Lord I know when we pray you answer in
three ways, yes, no, or wait. When we have to
wait Lord it hurts, sometimes the waiting is long
We know we must not help you in the process of
Waiting, that's why I am waiting on you

Strengthen me Lord while I wait am waiting
You know my thoughts, you know and see
every step I make Lord I am waiting for my
blessings for I know you will come through
for me. You never fail me yet. I am waiting
Lord for my blessings.

Praise the Lord

Psalm 98 verse 4 said, "make a joyful noise unto the Lord all the earth". Make a loud noise and rejoice and sing praise

You don't have to have faith to praise the Lord it's something you choose to do. Whether you are in the wilderness or in the promise land, you can praise him. Praise the Lord praise him.

If you are on the mountain top or in the valley, you can praise him it's your choice. When praises go up blessings come down. Praise move the hand of God. Praise the Lord praise him.

Things start to happened when we praise the Lord. He inhabits the praise of his people. He is worthy of our praise. We have not tongues enough to praise him. Praise the Lord praise him.

He didn't throw the clay away

Our God made man, he blow his breath in man and man became a living soul. But man disobeyed God and fall into sin. We have to confess our sins to God and he will forgive. Thank you Lord you didn't throw the clay away.

God set out his laws for man to do but man disobeyed and turn his own way, sink deeper and deeper into sin. God in his loving kindness said come unto me and I will give you rest. He didn't throw the clay away.

God never threw the clay away oh no no no he didn't throw the clay away. He never leave us alone. We are the ones that stray from him. He said come back home my child then you will make the right choice. He didn't throw the clay away.

When I speak your name

Oh Jesus when I speak your name, there is power, peace, joy and love. I want to know more about you Lord, you are so awesome. O Jesus I cannot describe your wonder. When I speak your name, there is peace in my soul.

Oh Jesus! Oh Jesus! You are so wonderful to me When I speak your name you bring peace to my soul. When I speak your name, am never the same. When I speak your name am closer drawn to you.

Oh father thank you for sending your son to die. Jesus you know your destiny but you came anyhow and very soon you are going to burst the clouds of heaven and bring lasting peace to the earth.

When I speak your name the enemy have to flee/ When I speak oh when I speak your name my body is healed and you supply my needs. When I speak your name my sins are forgiven. Jesus I love I love to call your name.

Jesus Cried

From the cross where Jesus died, he cried, "it's finished." He said father into your hands I commit my spirit. His face shone like the glory of the sun. Then he bowed his head upon his chest and died, and through his death we have hope of external life.

Oh the terror and blessings at Jesus death. The anguish and the pain he bore. Our sins nailed him to the cross and through his death we have hope of external life. He died to save us from sin just trust him today.

Jesus cried, it is finished, then he bowed his head and died There was a violent earthquake. The people were terrified, the rocks rented asunder, sepulchers were open, and dead bodies were seen and rose at his resurrection. Oh… what a scene

When Jesus cried it is finished, the priest was about to slay the lamb for sacrifice. The knife fell from his hand, and the lamb ran away. My friends type met antitype in the death of God's son. Jesus became sacrifice for us. Thank you Jesus for dying for me.

Take a look at Calvary

Jesus died alone on that cruel cross. He died the most shameful death. He did it for you and for me. With no garment thrown around him, his blood covered his shame He died because he loved us so. Thank you Jesus for dying for me.

Wake up! Wake up! People of the world
take a look at Calvary! See our savior died
he died that we might live. Thank you Jesus
for your love. The word said, the saved ones
will meet you in the air and you take it from there

Why father why, why did you allow your son to die such a shameful death? That's an answer we may not know, but I thank you father for letting your son go What would we do Jesus if you didn't die. Thank you Jesus for coming to earth.

Thank you Jesus that you didn't stay on the cross, you were buried, you didn't stay in the grave. You rose again and we can look up to heaven for you are now our high priest making intersession for us. Thank you Lord for the promise of your second coming.

Jesus is always on time

Lord Jesus you are always on time
When Lazerus died you waited four days
Before you go on the seen. Martha said Lord!
If you were here my brother would not died
Jesus you were four days late but on time

Four days late but on time
Jesus you have your reason for the delay
You let the people see that you work with
the impossible and a miracle is possible
four days late but on time

There is power in the name of Jesus,
life, healing, joy, and peace. Mary and
Martha were glad when you raise Lazerus
from the dead. Jesus, you are the greatest
miracle worker and you are always on time

Jesus is always on time. Don't give up on
your problems. When the way seems dark
before you, have faith and wait. Jesus will
come through for you. He is always on time.
Always on time.

Get on your knees

Fight all your battles on your knees and you will win
all the time. Don't wait until when trouble comes to pray.
Get on your knees and pray for when you get on your
knees, the devil will have to flee.

When we get on our knees the devil will leave us alone.
Don't let the enemy win. Jesus always have the answer
and he have the last move. Keep on praying until lights
break through, just trust him today.

Jesus never force no one to come to him, its your choice
You have to pray to the father through Jesus the son
Just get on your knees you'll find the answer on your
knees, on your knees

Light of the world

Jesus when you stepped down into the darkness
there was light. You are the light of the world. You
only speak the word and the work was done. You
are the light of the world.

Jesus you are the light of the world. When you came
into this world you became our light. You became sin
for us when you died on Calvary. You are the light of
the world.

Oh Calvary dark Calvary, that's where my savior
died for me. Thank you Jesus for stepping down
into this dark world of sin. You are light of the world.

Lord hear my cry

Lord hear my cry, hold my hand
hold my hand lest I fall. Out of the
depths have I cried onto thee. Keep
me safe Lord, please hear my cry,
hear my call lest I fall.

Dear Lord my trust is in thee
Please give me your shoulder,
Yes your broad shoulder to lean
on because there is no one like you.
Lord you've been my guide throughout
my life and I know Lord Jesus you won't
let me fall.

Oh "my precious savior"
hold my hand lest I fall
I know I can depend on thee
O my kind savior please stand
by me hold my hand lest I fall.

33

The Master of the sea

Look at the ocean how deep and wide oh
Lord how great thou art. You parted the red
sea, the children of Israel go over on dry land
You are the master of the sea.

The parting of the red sea, oh! What a God
One of the greatest miracle O Lord how great
thou art. The master of the sea you are. There
is no one like you.

I love to watch the waves overlapping each other
In the sea Lord, you provided fish for man to eat
You allow the ships and the boats to ride on the
waters. You are the Master of the sea.

All the rivers run in the sea and it never overflows.
O Lord you make the sand for its borders. The sea
cleanses itself. We bathe in it even for our healing.
You are the Master of the sea.

Keep the Sabbath Holy

Search for the truth in the Bible and you will find
the answer. The Lord said remember "my" Sabbath
to keep it holy. Obedience is better than sacrifice, make
the right choice for he said keep my Sabbath holy.

God's holy words are true, search, search the scriptures
be obedient and trust him. The seventh day is the Sabbath
of the Lord, he said keep my Sabbath holy. He said I am
God and there is none like me.

We must be obedient to the Lord and take him at his word.
O holy Sabbath day of rest, God's words are good, kind and
true. In Hebrews four he said if I have given you another day
I would have told you.

The Sabbath is not ours it's the Lord. He said, keep my
sabbath holy and we will reap the joy of the earth. The
Lord wants us to keep his day holy. Be obedient my friends
and take him at his word.

God's Holy Day

God design his holy day of rest. He said remember to keep my day holy. He knows that we would forget that's why he said remember to keep my Sabbath holy. Trust him today and take him at his word.

The Sabbath was from the beginning. In Genesis two verse three God rested on the seventh day, not because he was tired. Creation was finished so he rested and we must rest too.

From Genesis to Revelation you can read about God's commandments which includes the Sabbath. Man thinks to change the Sabbath but it is still binding. It's one of the ten commandments. He said keep my day holy.

My friends don't take God words simple. He means what he said. Keeping the Sabbath and the other commandments cannot save you, but we all must be obedient and take God at his word.

All is not lost

When you think you lost everything, remember God is still God and he never fails. Just trust him today he will make the way. He cares for you, for all is not lost.

All is not lost, just open up your eyes, look around you don't you see you are standing on top of the earth and you are not laying in the grave. Whilst there is life there is hope…won't you trust the Lord today.

You may lose your home, you may lose your job
You may lose your health and other things. You may
Be crying right now. God send his son to die for you
He said my child for you tears I died.

Father, Mother, you may not know where the next meal is coming from. You may be out in the cold right now, cry out to God he cares for you. All is not lost, all is not lost.

I have lost many things in my life. I lost many loved ones. I am getting older and older each day. There I lost my beauty. But thank God I never lost my mind nor I never lost my hope in God. Never lost my faith…he delivered me.

The Mountains and the Walls

With God's strength you can climb the highest mountain
With the mountains, there are rocks and trees to
hold on and by faith in God you can make it over. God is
So good just trust him today.

When you are facing the walls, God is right there.
Remember, when you are on top of the mountain,
you are facing the valley. In the valley that's where
your faith is tried. God is the same God in all these
situations. Trust him today he will carry you through.

The wall is different from the mountain. You cannot
climb it. You have to go around it. Just like the walls
of Jerico, give a shout and a praise to God. He will take
it down for you.

The walls and the mountains may be sickness
in your body, may be a financial need, a disobedient
child or you may lost a loved one. God is still God
He will take you through them all.

The Bitter Cup

Jesus you drank the bitter cup that no one on earth
or in heaven could ever dear to taste. That bitter cup
is your death on Calvary. You did it once and for all

Jesus, your death on Calvary was for the sins of the
whole world. You see that we were lost in sin and
you chose to drink that bitter cup. Thank you Jesus
for dying for me.

Jesus when you was in Gethsemane you prayed
to the Father. You said father if it be possible let
this cup pass from me not my will but let your
will be done. You drank that bitter cup for me.

Thank you Jesus for drinking that bitter cup
Thank you father for letting your son go. Jesus
You willing gave your life for us on Calvary
O Calvary that's where my savior died.

The Olive Tree

When problems come my way and needs arise in my life
When the way seems dark before me. When the olive tree
shall fail and there is no fruit in the vine. O Lord please help
me to trust you.

Though the olive tree shall fail and there is no fruit
in the vine O Lord by your grace I will praise you.
I will praise you. Please give me the faith to go on.

All praise and glory to you O Lord
You never fail me yet. You are my provider.
There is light at the end of the tunnel and you
will come through for me. You are my friend and
guide. You never fail me yet.

O Lord please help me to stand up for you, to trust
You even in the darkest night even when I don't know
what the outcome may be. You promise to protect your
people and I know you never fail

Give me the Bible

The holy bible is a gift from God. It is the road map to eternity. When my heart is broken, give me the bible. It's the way of salvation. It's God's gift to man.

Read the bible you'll get knowledge and understanding God's holy words are true. Give me the bible give me the bible. It's God's gift to man. Read it and be saved.

My friends read the bible. God promises are in the Psalms. Read the gospels. His promises are there. Read the proverbs and Isiah. From Genesis to revelation its doctrines are holy.

Amos 8:11 said, the Lord will send a thirst on the land, not for water or bread, but of hearing the word. The bible contains the mind of God. Read it to be wise. Believe it to be safe.

How great is our God

Our great God is still God. He never changed.
God from the beginning, God now and God
throughout eternity, that's who he is. He said
I am God and there is none like me.

Oh how great is our God. He is ever the same.
God from the beginning, God now and throughout
eternity. Oh God how great thou art. You are worthy
to be praise.

Our great God, the mighty one who made heaven and
earth through his son Jesus Christ. The great I am
the holy one. God of all Gods how great thou art.

How great is our God. He is so good. He gives man
knowledge to do many things. We must thank him,
praise him, and worship him. Oh God how great thou art.

Come see a man

The woman of Samaria the woman, she went to Jacob's well that day. She went to draw she met Jesus there. Jesus said, give me to drink. She said how are you a Jew ask a woman of Samaria for water. Jesus said if you know who I am you would ask of me and I would give you living water and you will never thirst again.

Jesus secured her attention and created her desires. Jesus said, if I give you this water you will never thirst again. She said give me that water. Jesus said go call your husband. She said I have none. Jesus said you have five and the one you now have is not yours. She went and tell others and said come see a man.

My friends Jesus see's all we do. He hears all we say. We cannot hide from him. Be conscious of your attitude just like the woman of the well. Jesus secured her attention. He created her desire and brought a conviction, then action followed. She went and tell others. She said come see a man...could this be the Christ?

43

Fear not what man can do

O Lord this world is filled with trouble, violence, sickness and disease. You said in your words that the heart of man is desperately wicked. Help us Lord not to be afraid what man can do, but to fear and trust only thee.

Precious savior, the whole world is in your hands. I know you are coming soon and whatever man may do or say will not stop you from coming. Fear not my child what man can do I can hear my savior say. Jesus you are going to burst the eastern skies and come take over your world.

My Jesus what a day that will be when we shall see you face to face and our loved ones we shall see. Hallelujah dear Lord what a glorious day that will be. Thank you Father for sending your only son to deliver sinful man from sin. Help us to trust and fear only thee.

To purchase a copy of my musical CD,
"The Love of God",

Please e-mail
Dwight.francis70@gmail.com

or call the following numbers,
(954) 599-4762 and (954) 234-5942.